SOUTHERN

CROSSINGS

A memento of your
visit to New Zealand
April 96

SUITE C, 177 PARNELL ROAD, PRIVATE BAG 93 23, PARNELL, AUCKLAND, NEW ZEALAND.
TELEPHONE 64-9-309 5912 (24 HOURS) FAX 64-9-377 5960

ARRANGERS OF EXCLUSIVE EXPERIENCES IN NEW ZEALAND, AUSTRALIA AND THE SOUTH PACIFIC

THE NEW ZEALAND EXPERIENCE

T H E
NEW ZEALAND
EXPERIENCE

Photographs by
WARREN JACOBS

Text by
JOHN WILSON

Kowhai Publishing Limited

Published in 1988 by Kowhai Publishing Ltd.
10 Peacock Street, Auckland, 299 Moorhouse Ave, Christchurch
Photographs copyright © Warren Jacobs Photography Ltd.
Reproduction of the whole or any part of the contents without written permission is prohibited
Design Warren Jacobs
Final artwork Graeme Hobbs
Typsetting Saba Graphics Ltd
Printing LeeFung Asco printers, China
ISBN 0 908598 34 3

CONTENTS

Endpaper:
South Canterbury

Page 2-3:
Yachts, Bay of Islands

NEW ZEALAND

New Zealand is not, by area, a large country. Its almost 270,000 square kilometres make it about the same size as the State of Colorado, Japan or Great Britain. But in that area are an astonishing variety of landscapes and climates, and an astonishing variety, therefore, of things to do. The "New Zealand Experience" is an amalgam of the many hundreds of possible experiences that a varied terrain and different weather conditions in a relatively small area make possible.

One reason for the country's great variety in a small area is its long, narrow shape. From Cape Reinga in the far north to Stewart Island's South Cape is about 1600 kilometres. A span of a comparable distance in Europe would put Cape Reinga in the Mediterranean and South Cape in the English Midlands. In North America you would need to travel from Memphis to Quebec, or from San Diego to Seattle, to cover the same distance. Cape Reinga lies on what feels like the southern edge of the tropical Pacific. Standing on South Cape, or even on Bluff Hill, when a southerly is howling you can be very aware indeed that only the empty, wind-tossed waters of the Great Southern Ocean lie between southern New Zealand and Antarctica.

New Zealand is sparsely populated, with only a few more than three million people in an area which contains, in Britain, more than fifty million and, in Japan, more than one hundred million. The country's relative lack of population is particularly marked south of Auckland. The South Island has fewer than one million people (about one quarter of the country's population) although the South Island is slightly larger than the North. The country's small population has its disadvantages. The old jibe that New Zealand closes down at the weekend is no longer fair — reasonable if not generous liquor licensing laws, Saturday shopping and a population more attuned than in past decades to the "outside world" have made sure of that. But it would be misleading to tout New Zealand's cities as comparable to larger cities overseas for urban experiences. There is an interesting cultural and urban life in New Zealand (80 per cent of the country's population lives in large town and cities) but you need to know where and when to look for it and not expect the continuous and varied activities that cities in other countries (even Australia) offer. However, even the great majority of New Zealanders who are urban dwellers tend to look beyond the cities and towns, to the sea, rivers, lakes, bushed hills and mountains, for their recreation.

Here the country's relatively sparse population is an advantage. New Zealand is incomparable for opportunities to enjoy solitude, engage in vigorous outdoor activities or experience nature almost unmodified. The country's many freedoms — to swim in almost any river or lake, for example, or to walk along almost any beach — are enshrined in law and are a precious part of the inheritance of New Zealanders. And the freedoms are shared, willingly, with visitors who come to experience things which are uniquely New Zealand's.

Department of Survey &
Land Information
Map Licence 1988/51
Crown Copyright Reserved.

Three Kings Islands

Spirits Bay
Cape Reinga
Cape Maria van Diemen
North Cape
Te Kao
Cape Karikari
Doubtless Bay
Mangonui
Ahipara Bay
Ninety Mile Beach
Awanui
Ahipara
Kaitaia
Karikari
Okahu
Kaikohe
Kawakawa
Moerewa
Cape Brett
Bay of Islands
Russell
Upper

Hokianga Harbour
Hikurangi
Whangarei
Portland

Dargaville
Te Kopuru
Waiotira
Waipu
Hen & Chickens Is
Maungaturoto
Ruawai
Little Barrier I
Port Fitzroy
Wellsford
Great Barrier I
Warkworth
Kawau I

Kaipara Harbour
Helensville
Mercury Is
Coromandel
Hauraki Gulf
Takapuna
Mercury Bay
AUCKLAND
Devonport
Whitianga
Papatoetoe
Coromandel
MANUKAU
Papakura
Thames
Peninsula
Manukau Harbour
Waiuku
Pukekohe
Whangamata
Tuakau
Meremere
Mayor Is
Waikato River
Te Kauwhata
Waihi
Huntly
Paeroa
Ngaruawahia
Waitoa
Mount Maunganui
Raglan
Morrinsville
Matakana I
Motiti I
White I
Raglan Harbour
HAMILTON
Matamata
Tauranga
Cambridge
Te Puke
Edgecumbe
Kawhia Harbour
Te Awamutu
Tirau
Kawerau
Bay of Plenty
Cape Runaway
Hicks Bay
Te Kaha
Te Araroa
East Cape

NORTH ISLAND

Otorohanga
Putaruru
Ngongotaha
Rotorua
Hikurangi 1754
Ruatoria
Te Kuiti
Kihikihi
Mangakino
Atiamuri
1111
Mt Tarawera
Te Puia
Mangakino
Reporoa
Te Whaiti
Tokomaru Bay
Tirua Point
Piopio
Kinleith
Murupara
Te Karaka
Tolaga Bay

Awakino
Mokau
Mokau River
Taumarunui
Waikino
Taupo
Lake Taupo
Turangi
Manutahi
Gisborne
Poverty Bay

Waitara
1968
Tongariro
Ngauruhoe 2291
New Plymouth
Inglewood
National Park
Ruapehu
RUAHINE RA
Dakou
Okato
Whakapapa
Chateau
Ohakune
Bay View
Wairoa
Cape Egmont
Mt Egmont 2518
Stratford
Raetihi
Waiouru
Napier
Mahia Peninsula
Kaponga
Eltham
Hastings
Hawke Bay
Rahotu
Normanby
Taihape
Havelock North
Opunake
Manaia
Hawera
Mangaweka
Waipawa
Cape Kidnappers
Patea
Waverley
Marton
Waipukurau
Dannevirke
Patea River
Hunterville
Bulls
Feilding
Danson
Porangahau
Wanganui
Ashhurst
Woodville
Rangitikei River
PALMERSTON NORTH
Pahiatua
Cape Turnagain
Manawatu River
Foxton
Waitarere
Shannon
RUAHINE RA
Eketahuna
Levin
Otaki
Castlepoint
Cape Farewell
Waikanae
Masterton
Farewell Spit
Collingwood
Kapiti I
Paraparaumu
Carterton
Golden Bay
Paekakariki
Featherston
Cape Stephens
Takaka
Porirua
Martinborough
D'Urville I
COOK
Tawa
Palliser Bay
Riwaka
Tasman Bay
Motueka
Picton
Upper Hutt
STRAIT
LOWER HUTT
Karamea
Havelock
Cape Palliser
Richmond
WELLINGTON
Wakefield
Nelson
Blenheim
Granity
Owen River
Renwick
Seddon

Buller River
Cape Foulwind
Westport
Murchison
St Arnaud
Ward
Cape Campbell
Inangahua Jnc
Mt Travers 2338
Punakaiki
Reefton
Maruia
Lewis
KAIKOURA
Mt Tapuaenuku 2885
Barrytown
Ikamatua
Springs Jnc
Pass
Clarence River
Blackball
Hanmer
Kaikoura
Grey River
Runanga
Brunner
Kumara
Springs
Greymouth
Lake Brunner
Waiau
Parnassus
Wiau River
Hokitika
Kaniere
Culverden
Cheviot
Ross
SOUTHERN
Arthur's Pass
Waikari
Hurunui River
Arthur's Pass
Waiau
Hawarden

SOUTH ISLAND

Abut Head
Whataroa
Harihari
Amberley
ALPS
Oxford
Rangiora
Lake Coleridge
Springfield
Franz Josef Glacier
Kaiapoi
Fox Glacier
Pegasus Bay
Belfast
Bruce Bay
3764
Mt Somers
CHRISTCHURCH
Mt Cook
Darfield
Lyttelton
Hermitage
Rolleston
Banks
Rakaia
Leeston
Lincoln
Peninsula
Southbridge
Akaroa
Jackson Bay
Mt Cook
Mt Dobson
Lake Ellesmere
Jackson Head
Ashburton
Rakaia River
Awarua Pt
Hinds
Mt Aspiring 3027
Canterbury
Lake Pukaki
Fairlie
Bight
Milford Sound
Wanaka
Geraldine
Mitre Peak 1692
Lake Tekapo
Temuka
Rangitata River
Bligh Sound
Homer Tunnel
Pleasant Point
Washdyke
George Sound
Milford Sound
Timaru
Glenorchy
Pareora
Caswell Sound
Arrowtown
Omarama
Queenstown
Cromwell
Doubtful Sound
Otematata
Waimate
Kingston
Clyde
Waitaki River
Te Anau
Wanaka
Alexandra
Oamaru
Resolution I
Manapouri
Hampden
Dusky Sound
Roxburgh
Palmerston
Chalky Inlet
Ohai
Nightcaps
Tuatapere
Lumsden
Waikouaiti
Puysegur Point
Riverdale
Lawrence
Otago Peninsula
Te Anau
Tapanui
Green Island
Port Chalmers
Mossburn
Clinton
Milton
DUNEDIN
Orepuki
Gore
Waipahi
Otautau
Mataura
Balclutha
Winton
Edendale
Kaitangata
Clutha River
Thornbury
Waikiwi
Wyndham
Owaka
INVERCARGILL
Riverton
Tokanui
Bluff
Solander I
FOVEAUX STRAIT
Ruapuke I
Mataura River

Mason Bay
Halfmoon Bay

Southwest Cape
STEWART ISLAND

The Snares

7

THE WARM NORTH
Northland and Auckland

The northern peninsulas of New Zealand — Northland itself, which reaches beyond Auckland to its dramatic end at Cape Reinga, and the smaller Coromandel Peninsula east of Auckland — are both, at least at their summer best, almost subtropical. The peninsula of Northland is larger than most New Zealanders themselves realise. To reach Cape Reinga by road from Auckland involves a journey of 450 kilometres.

The warm-water beaches of Northland and the Coromandel afford opportunities for swimming, fishing and yachting (in New Zealand even the smallest sailboat is commonly called a yacht). The coasts of both peninsulas are the playgrounds of New Zealand's largest concentration of population — greater Auckland, which about one million people call home.

The sea dominates the northern parts of New Zealand almost as much as it dominates life in the tropical Pacific islands to the north. Auckland itself is all but an island, the Waitemata and Manakau Harbours fingering round the isthmus of old volcanic cones on which the city was built. Auckland's population, too, underlines the strength of the the links which the northern parts of New Zealand have with the tropical Pacific. Auckland is the world's largest Polynesian city, in the sense that more Polynesians — Cook Islanders, Samoans, Tongans, Niueans, Tokelauans — live there than anywhere else.

But there is more than the sea and beautiful beaches to Northland and the Coromandel. West of Auckland, the Waitakere Ranges raise blue-green, bush-covered slopes to a high undulating crest and the Coromandel Peninsula has a high forested spine which can be explored on foot. Though most of Northland has been stripped of its original cover of magnificent kauri trees and its interior hills and ranges are now farmland or sometimes unattractive scrub, there are many pockets of natural and historical beauty.

Aucklanders are often heard to say "South of the Bombay Hills . . ." and leave it at that, implying that the rest of New Zealand hardly counts. More than one-third of the country's population lives north of that "frontier", but they are living a good distance from the best scenery and opportunities for recreation that the country offers. Much of the finest scenery and most of the opportunities for different sorts of outdoor recreation are found further south, though even southerners will concede that the North's beaches and boating waters cannot be beaten.

In 1769 Captain Cook, New Zealand's European rediscoverer, found the fretted coastline and island-studded waters of the Bay of Islands (left) one of the country's most attractive anchorages. Soon afterwards, on the shores of the Bay, occurred one of the first sustained contacts between Europeans and the indigenous Maori people. The combination of historic interest and opportunities for sailing, swimming or fishing makes the Bay of Islands one of New Zealand's most popular resort areas. In high summer, towns like Paihia, Russell or Kerikeri are alive with holiday-makers. The towns settle back into somnolence in winter, but even then southerners escape to the Bay of Islands from their harsher season.

Most New Zealanders refer to the native forest which originally covered most of New Zealand as "bush". But you never hear of "kauri bush" only "kauri forest", an indication of the stature of New Zealand's most magnificent tree which grew only north of a line not far south of Auckland. The kauri (left) was quickly exploited to provide superb masts and spars for sailing ships and later as a superior building timber. Between the 1820s and the early years of this century, the kauri trade was of great importance to the city of Auckland. The price of this was the stripping of most of Northland of its fine forests. Pockets of former magnificence have been preserved and are now jealously protected. The largest surviving kauri forest is at Waipoua, on Northland's west coast.

In early February 1840, a large number of Maori chiefs gathered in front of the house of the British Resident at Waitangi (top right) on the shores of the Bay of Islands for one of the most momentous days in New Zealand's history, 6 February 1840, when the Treaty of Waitangi was signed between Hobson, New Zealand's first British Governor, and the assembled Maori. Many New Zealanders — Pakeha and Maori — believe that the Treaty has been more honoured in the breach than in the observance. But all acknowledge its importance as a symbol of the equal partnership between the races that is the foundation of New Zealand's national identity, even if the partnership is not yet as equal as it should be.

The presence of a large Maori population in the Kerikeri area prompted the founding there, in 1819, of New Zealand's second mission station. Three old buildings at the Kerikeri Basin (right) are reminders of this chapter in Kerikeri's past. The Kemp House, right, New Zealand's oldest building, was completed in 1822. The Stone Store, left, was built 1832-35. Between the two, on a small rise, the Church of St James, built in 1878, is a relative youngster. People come to the Kerikeri Basin for its history and its tranquillity.

Visitors from overseas, and New Zealanders who have travelled, often marvel at the easy access New Zealanders enjoy to superb beaches that in more populous countries would be crowded with holidaymakers or the private preserve of people owning the land. Here the grey sand and warm waters of Whale Bay (left) are being enjoyed, even at the height of the holiday season, by just a handful of people.

The improvement of Northland's roads and the concentration of economic activity in Whangarei and Auckland have drained life out of many of the region's small towns. Mangonui (top right) was once an important port from which kauri timber was shipped. It survives now as a farming service and tourist centre, and because many retired people find it an attractive place to live.

Off the northern coasts of New Zealand is some of the finest deep-sea fishing in the world. But not everyone aspires to hook a swordfish from the deck of a launch out in the open sea. In small rowing boats, families will set off from pebbly beaches like Rawhiti (right) with line or net with nothing more in mind than a few lazy hours on the water and the hope that they may bring their evening meal home with them.

13

BAY OF ISLANDS SWORDFISH
CLUB
15·2·86
ANGLER BRENT JOHNSON
FISH S/MARLIN
WEIGHT 102 KGS 224·8 lb
TACKLE 37 KG. B/S
LAUNCH PILADO
JUNIOR ANGLER

The American writer Zane Grey was the first to bring international acclaim to the superb deep-sea fishing off northern New Zealand. From the Bay of Plenty north to the Bay of Islands, people set out from small ports in powerful launches, with striped marlin (left) the most prized catch.

Many generations of New Zealand children have spent happy hours fishing from countless small wharves in bays around the country's long coastline. These children (above) are at Whitianga, an important holiday centre on Mercury Bay, which is on the outer side of the Coromandel Peninsula. But they could as well be at any coastal town from Mangonui in the north to Stewart Island's Golden Bay in the south.

Two oceans meet in swirling currents and eddies beyond the tip of Cape Reinga (right), the Tasman Sea to the left and the South Pacific to the right. The scenery is dramatic. But Cape Reinga is also recognised by New Zealanders as a place of spiritual power. New Zealand's "land's end" is also where, in Maori belief, the spirits of the dead took their departure from the land of the living, descending beneath the sea down the roots of an old gnarled pohutukawa which still clings to the cliffs of the Cape. The Cape is a reminder of other journeys too, for it beckons north into the Pacific, towards the tropical islands from which New Zealand's first settlers sailed, more than a millennium ago.

Even in the colder southern cities, Wellington, Christchurch and Dunedin, enthusiastic "boaties" are out on local harbours on every favourable weekend. But Auckland — sometimes referred to as "the city of sails" — is undoubtedly the centre of New Zealand yachting, with superb sailing on the Waitemata Harbour (opposite) within sight of the tall buildings of the downtown.

The construction boom of recent years has given downtown Auckland (left) the appearance of a world city. In the green patch of Albert Park, buildings of an older Auckland survive among trees. In the middle distance, the Harbour is spanned by the bridge which was opened in 1959 and now carries a flood of commuters from the populous North Shore suburbs into the city.

Thirty years ago, the inner Auckland suburb of Parnell (below) was in decline. It is now one of the trendiest places to live in Auckland. Central to the reversal of the suburb's decline was the creation of Parnell Village. An enterprising developer linked a number of older houses into an exciting shopping centre. Parnell Village, and similar developments in other cities, provide the greater variety and sophistication in shopping which New Zealanders now demand.

The sing-song drone of the racing commentator is a familiar weekend sound in suburban New Zealand as people tune in to discover if a fortune has been made. The local TAB, where off-course bets can be placed, often draws larger crowds on a Saturday than a nearby church will draw the next day. There are separate racecourses for galloping (top) and pacing in all the country's major cities and towns and many small centres have courses for occasional meetings. Horse breeding is a major pursuit in New Zealand and a day at the races an important event in many family calendars.

Rugby may no longer be New Zealand's national religion, but sport still looms large in the lives of many New Zealanders. Auckland's Stanley Street Courts (middle) are the venue for the most important of New Zealand's tennis matches which attract large crowds. New Zealand struggles to be considered a power in world tennis, but all schools and most towns as well as cities have tennis courts.

Overseas crazes seldom take long to reach New Zealand and windsurfing became a major sport here soon after it first became popular in Europe and North America. Young windsurfers had soon staked out certain beaches — like breezy Torpedo Bay (bottom) on Auckland's North Shore — as their particular preserve.

A barbecue on the beach (opposite) is almost a secular ritual in New Zealand, and living in the heart of Auckland city is no restraint on performing the ritual. Five or ten minutes from the downtown are bays where the men can char their sausages and burn their chops while the children play on the water's edge and the womenfolk chat after emptying their chilly bins.

New Zealand lacks a significant number of brightly coloured flowering native plants, but in summer the pohutukawa (above), known as the New Zealand Christmas tree, spangles northern coasts with its bright red flowers.

In 1769, not long after his first landfall in New Zealand, Captain Cook brought the "Endeavour" to anchor in Mercury Bay, (right) where his party observed the transit of Mercury. While at anchor in Mercury Bay, Cook made his first prolonged contact with the Maori people. The waters of the bay are admired today chiefly for their beauty, but their importance as the scene of "a pivotal moment in the history of our nation" also draws holidaymakers to the bay.

A HIGH HEARTLAND
The Central North Island

South from Auckland, State Highway 1 passes through rolling country, then crosses somewhat steeper hills before dropping to meet the Waikato River, about 30 kilometres east of the river's mouth. The Waikato River, at 425 kilometres New Zealand's longest, has its source high in the centre of the North Island. It flows through Lake Taupo, largest of New Zealand's lakes, then north down the centre of the North Island towards the rich Waikato lowlands.

Chief city of these lowlands is Hamilton, one of New Zealand's fastest growing centres in recent years. The fertile lowlands have little in common, geographically, with the more barren volcanic interior of the island, but the Waikato River provides an historical and topographical link between the areas. The river was sacred to the Maori tribes which lived along its banks and a wealth of legends about it have survived. The Waikato lowlands were one of the areas over which Maori and Pakeha fought for possession last century giving the region a legacy of warfare which most parts of New Zealand lack.

East and a little south of the lower Waikato lies Rotorua. Rotorua's link with the high centre of the island is the belt of geothermal activity that reaches from the summits of the central volcanoes right out to sea at White Island off the Bay of Plenty Coast. The thermal activity is itself one of the area's attractions — Rotorua's boiling mud, simmering springs and spouting geysers have drawn visitors for many decades. The vitality of Maori culture in the thermal region has been another of its attractions.

The terrain of the central North Island, though dramatic only where the central volcanoes thrust upwards, is varied and so too are the activities possible in the area. The terrain ranges from lofty mountains, through semi-deserts and high pumice plains, through broken hill country down to the lowland or coastal flats of the lower Waikato and Bay of Plenty. The central volcanoes provide the North Island's best skiing. The slopes of the bulkiest of the mountains, Ruapehu, have excellent facilities. The often tempestuous rivers offer exciting canoeing or rafting, although the mightiest of the rivers, the Waikato itself, has been tamed for most of its length by hydro dams. The higher ranges, now surrounded by farmland or exotic forests, are still forested and present opportunities for tramping and shooting.

The region's main centres are Hamilton, Rotorua, Tauranga, Whakatane and Taupo. Apart from these cities, the central North Island is very much small town country, with often little more than a pub and a store standing where the maps mark a local centre.

Visitors to Rotorua tread gingerly, for everywhere are reminders of how thin and fragile the earth's crust is. Colourful mineral deposits add to the attraction of the Champagne Pool's bubbling, crystalline water (left). But the most magnificent of the country's mineral deposits, the silica Pink and White Terraces, were destroyed more than a hundred years ago by a volcanic eruption.

24

Much of the land of the central North Island proved poor farmland. But introduced trees, notably pinus radiata from California, like the poor pumice soils and grow faster in New Zealand than in their original habitats. Forests now clothe vast tracts of the central North Island and feed important pulp and paper and timber industries. Here some of the exotic forests are seen across the waters of the Maraetai hydro lake (far left), not far from the hydro construction town of Mangakino.

The Waikato River (top left) was an important line of communication for the Maori and for the first European settlers. Great canoes were the prized possessions of the riverside tribes and later gunboats on the river were an important advantage to the British Army in the wars of the 1860s. Today's river traffic is more peaceful. Canoes are brought out for annual regattas at Ngaruawahia and pleasure trips can be taken on an old paddlewheel steamer where the river flows through Hamilton.

To use the prodigious quantities of wood produced in the exotic forests of the central North Island, giant mills have been built at Kawerau and Tokoroa to produce pulp and paper, logs and sawn timber, much for export. New Zealand often presents a curious juxtaposition of the rural and the industrial. In the picture (opposite below) Friesan dairy cows, the country's most popular breed, graze close to the huge Kinleith Mill which covers 233 hectares, employs about 4000 workers and works night and day.

New Zealand has extensive areas of limestone which are riddled with caves. Among the largest, and the only ones in the North Island extensively developed for tourism, are the caves at Waitomo (left) in the hills of the King Country. The caves are renowned for spectacular glow worms as well as impressive limestone formations. The caves were first opened to tourists soon after their exploration in the 1880s. Adventuresome New Zealand speleologists venture into partially explored caves in other parts of the country. The only other major caves developed for tourism are far to the south, on the shores of Lake Te Anau.

25

For much of its length below Lake Taupo, the Waikato River is now a series of hydro lakes, its waters impounded by high dams. One of these lakes, Karapiro (top), which lies just to the east of Cambridge and is easily accessible from Hamilton, has a world class rowing course. It is used by school-boys as well as the top rowers who have won renown for New Zealand in international competition.

Most of New Zealand's smaller towns are rural service centres, with shops and administrative services for farmers from the surrounding countryside and perhaps some local industry. Most, too, like Cambridge (above), take pride in their appearance and despite the economic downturn in New Zealand farming in the 1980s, still manage to present a prosperous, established air to visitors. At the end of the street is the war memorial, a familiar feature in all towns, large and small, of a country which this century sent thousands of men and women away to fight overseas.

The commonest farm animal in the Waikato is the dairy cow. But the Waikato is also an important centre of horse breeding. These horses grazing contentedly on a Waikato stud farm (right) are evidence of the large industry based on the popularity of horse racing in New Zealand.

These campers (left) on the Bay of Plenty coast are looking directly out to White Island, the island volcano which marks the furthest extent northwards of the central North Island's volcanic belt. Attempts to mine sulphur were frustrated by the island's continuous and sporadically violent activity. New Zealanders are inveterate campers, taking caravans and tents to spots by sea, river or lake where they relax through New Zealand's long, usually hot, summer break over Christmas and New Year.

Tauranga lies on the waters of a harbour whose name means "sheltered anchorage". Its near neighbour, Mount Maunganui (bottom) is also a major port and holiday resort. It presents one face to the open sea and powerful Pacific rollers attract surfers (top) to "The Mount" from all over the country. Mount Maunganui has a boisterous reputation for the summer weeks when young holiday makers crowd into town.

New Zealand's "villages" lack the venerable charm of European villages. The landscape is too raw and the country too recently settled for the little settlements to have merged comfortably with their surroundings. Pub and store, and perhaps tiny telephone exchange, almost invariably built of timber and corrugated iron, are often the only buildings, apart from a few houses, to make up a township. But they have an honest if untidy beauty about them and their settings, like that of Waihau Bay (middle) on the eastern Bay of Plenty coast, often make up for any deficiency in their architecture or appearance.

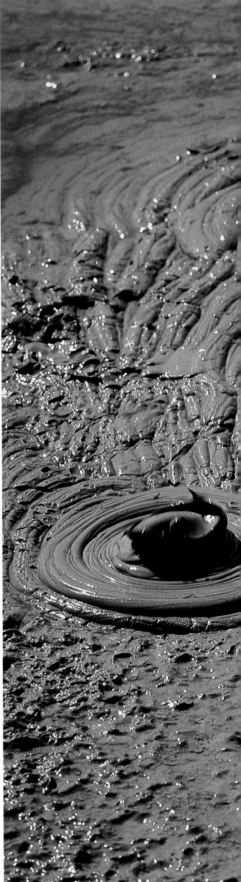

Several of New Zealand's geyser fields have been destroyed, foolishly some think, by flooding when the Waikato hydro lakes were filled or by use of steam in geothermal power stations. Concern that activity at Rotorua's Whakarewarewa field might also diminish has led to the imposition of curbs on the use of hot water from the ground by the city's homes and businesses. Pohutu, largest of New Zealand's geysers, (above) still throws its plume a spectacular 30 metres into the air.

One of the most intriguing sights in the thermal regions, a source of fascination to young New Zealanders living outside the thermal regions, is glutinous mud boiling (right) like porridge.

The culture of the Maori people has survived more than 150 years of European colonisation with extraordinary resilience and strength. The Maori are now about 12 per cent of the population, but the impact of their culture on New Zealand life is profound. Most tourists encounter Maori culture at places like Rotorua where perfomances give them a glimpse of Maori ways of life and belief. Though many New Zealanders regard these presentations of Maori culture as artificial, they do reflect the vibrant and vigorous culture preserved on hundreds of marae throughout the country. The protocol of the marae — the assembly points, often in front of a carved meeting house, where tribes or subtribes gather on important occasions — is still strictly maintained when visitors arrive. The challenge to the visitors is made by a warrior armed with a taiaha (opposite). The poi (below) is a form of ceremonial dance performed by women. Recent years have seen a renaissance of many Maori cultural practices. The Maori language is being fostered and Maori arts and crafts are being accorded new respect. The Maori are among the world's finest woodcarvers and this art is kept alive at the Maori Arts and Crafts Institute in Rotorua (left). The canoe prow is a traditional object, similar to many made by the young carver's ancestors for centuries before European settlement of New Zealand.

Last century, the New Zealand Government dreamed of New Zealand's thermal areas becoming important spa, attracting tourists from all over the world. The dream never came to fruition, but one legacy of it is Rotorua's grand "Tudor Towers" (above), first built in 1906-07 as a government bath house, but now used as a museum, art gallery and entertainment centre. Lawn bowls is a popular pastime among New Zealanders, especially the elderly, but New Zealanders of all ages can be found on the country's hundreds of greens.

New Zealand's largest lake, Taupo, (opposite) fills the vast crater of a gigantic volcanic explosion which, nearly 2000 years ago, blanketed large areas of the North Island with pumice and ash. The cataclysm left a fine legacy in the form of a broad stretch of water used for almost every conceivable form of water sport or boating. The North Island makes up for its relative lack of lakes compared with the South by having the country's largest. Taupo's 600 square kilometres make it nearly twice as big as the country's second largest lake, Te Anau.

At the southern end of Lake Taupo, (opposite) the Tongariro River meanders across its miniature delta. It is reputed to be one of the finest fishing rivers in the world. Turangi, once a sleepy fishing resort, grew markedly with the building of the Tongariro power scheme. But the Tongariro River survived these significant changes with its angling reputation intact.

Trout fishing in New Zealand is free, except for the relatively small amount that must be paid to the local acclimatisation societies for a licence. All comers can test their angling skills on stretches of water which elsewhere could well be the preserve of only the very rich. The Waitahanui Stream (above) is one of the many excellent fishing rivers which flow into Lake Taupo.

A fisherman (left) proudly displays proof of the excellence of the angling in the central North Island's rivers. Brown trout, coming from England via Tasmania, were introduced into New Zealand waters in 1868 and rainbow trout, from California, in 1884. Today, fish caught average between two and five pounds in weight, but much larger fish are there to test the angler's skill.

Ferns of hundreds of species, from tiny ground-hugging plants to giant tree ferns, are a notable feature of the New Zealand bush. The silver fern (above) which adorns the jerseys of the men who represent New Zealand at rugby football, is second only to the kiwi as a national symbol.

New Zealand lies almost exactly half way round the world from the Greenwich meridian. The international date line, where one day changes to the next, runs just to the east of New Zealand. Lofty Mount Hikurangi (top right) on the North Island's East Cape would be the first place in the world to greet the new day — except that the international date line kinks to allow the Chatham Islands, part of New Zealand, to be on the same day as the rest of the country.

The days when the horse was the main means of travel for New Zealanders are long gone. Even on farms, the trailbike has largely replaced the horse. But young people riding horses on shingle roads are still a common sight on the East Cape. Throughout the country, horse trek operations offer visitors and novices the opportunity to enjoy the relaxed pleasure these two young Maori at Lottin Point (right) take for granted.

New Zealand's main and secondary roads are generally sealed. But the typical New Zealand country remains narrow and metalled, ambling past lonely farmhouses in towards rugged hills. This view, (opposite) near Hikurangi, is a rural scene as typical of New Zealand as one could find anywhere in the country.

SOUTH TO THE CAPITAL
Hawkes Bay, Taranaki and Wellington

From the often turbulent waters of Cook Strait, a high spine of rugged mountains runs north to end, eventually, at Mount Hikurangi on the East Cape. In the southern half of the North Island, Hawkes Bay and the Wairarapa lie to the east of these ranges and the Manawatu and Rangitikei to the east. North of the Rangitikei and further east again, the high cone of Taranaki (Mount Egmont) dominates the province of Taranaki.

Napier serves as the port of Hawkes Bay and New Plymouth as the port of Taranaki, but most of the North Island south of the central plateau is the hinterland of Wellington, situated on a superb natural harbour at the very bottom of the North Island.

Hawkes Bay and the Wairarapa are largely hill country, with areas of flat plains lying between the ranges. These two regions are uncompromisingly rural — they epitomise the farming heartlands of the country and even the larger towns function primarily as rural service centres. There is little drama in the scenery, but pleasing rural landscapes abound.

Taranaki, by contrast, has one of New Zealand's most dramatic geographical features, the near symmetrical cone of a volcano the name of which has become something of an issue. Taranaki to the Maori who lived around its base, the mountain was renamed Egmont by Captain Cook. In recent years, a Maori resurgence has led to pressure to change the name back to its original Taranaki. The Geographical Board has compromised by giving both names equal status.

At the North Island's southern end, Wellington has been the country's capital since 1865 when the seat of government was shifted south from Auckland to be nearer the centre of the country and the then more prosperous and populous provinces of Canterbury and Otago. Wellington has an improbable site for a major city, let alone a capital. It is hemmed in by hills to the shores of a superb harbour and sits, alarmingly, astride a major fault line.

Wellington's dramatic setting and its being crowded between water and hills have given it a livelier urban culture than other major New Zealand centres, even larger Auckland, as if Wellingtonians, jostled close together by the geography of their city and denied the easy access to beaches and the sea enjoyed by Aucklanders or to the mountains enjoyed by those who live in Christchurch, have been obliged to make the city itself the main focus of their interests and activities.

The fertile flanks of Mount Taranaki/Egmont support intensive dairy farming. Inland from the mountain, the rest of the Taranaki Province is mostly rugged and steep hill country (left). More than a century ago the bush was cleared from these hills and pastures established which are now grazed by sheep and cattle, the basis of New Zealand's large meat industry. The musterer on horseback is still a reasonably common sight on New Zealand's backblock roads, though farm bikes have in many cases taken the place of the more picturesque horses.

Hawkes Bay's equitable climate has made it one of the prime horticultural areas of New Zealand. Fruit and vegetables are grown for canning or freezing in local factories or for distribution fresh throughout the country. And grapes are grown to help sustain New Zealand's fast expanding wine industry. Wine has been made in areas like Hawkes Bay (left) for many decades, but it is only in recent years that New Zealand wines have gained a reputation for quality and that grape growing has become a major industry.

The New Zealand countryside lacks castles and great country houses, but many find equal attraction in the hundreds of humbler, usually wooden, old farmhouses to be found in rural areas from Northland to Southland. The rapid growth of exotic trees has given this homestead near Waipukurau (top) a settled, established air, perhaps surprising in a country so young.

Many of Hawkes Bay's small rural towns have appealing old buildings. The butcher's shop at Onga Onga (above) is a particular favourite of many for the perfection of its miniature style. A beautifully restored Chevrolet truck completes a picture of period charm.

43

In 1931, New Zealand's most devastating earthquake shook Hawkes Bay. Large parts of Napier (top) were destroyed by the earthquake and the fires which followed. Quickly, though times were hard, Napier was rebuilt. Today the sun-drenched seaside city has a world reputation as a place to see fine Art Deco architecture.

Cape Kidnappers was given its present name by Captain Cook when a local Maori attempted to kidnap one of the "Endeavour's" crew. Its older name, Te Matau o Maui (Maui's Fish-hook), recalls the legend that the North Island was pulled up out of the sea by the culture hero, Maui. What draws visitors to Kidnappers today are thousands of gannets nesting on the white crest of the Cape. The birds are at the colony, which is believed to be the only mainland gannet colony in the world, from July through to April. In the picture (above) tourists who have travelled along the beach on tractor-drawn trailers have paused on their way to the Cape at the satellite colony on Black Reef.

Whitebait is a particular New Zealand delicacy — the young of various species of fish which swarm up rivers at certain seasons of the year. They are taken in large, fine nets suspended in the rivers close to their mouths. Here a family is placing its net in the Ngaruroro River, (right) in anticipation of a delicious meal of whitebait fritters.

44

New Zealand lies athwart the "roaring forties", the belt of almost ceaseless trade winds which circle the globe at New Zealand's latitudes. The winds can be trying, but off Taranaki's Cape Egmont (left) a hang-glider takes advantage of the prevailing westerly to soar high above beach and ocean. Like windsurfing, hang-gliding has gained great popularity in New Zealand in recent years.

New Zealand's east coast has one of the loneliest prospects of any coastline in the world. Look west from New Zealand and Australia is a mere 1600 kilometres away. Look east and it is 6000 kilometres to South America, across empty ocean. The Pacific breaking on the dark grey sand of Blacks Beach, Mahia, (above) at the northern end of Hawkes Bay captures this sense of New Zealand's lonely isolation in one corner of the world's largest ocean.

The popularity of golfing in New Zealand is evident in the large number of club and public golf courses throughout the country. Some are nine-hole courses built by locals for their own enjoyment, but others are full eighteen-hole courses of international standard. Playing golf in New Zealand means enjoying usually uncrowded greens and often beautiful rural settings. Here Mount Taranaki/Egmont (above) overlooks the players. Most New Zealand courses are club-owned, but visitors are welcome to play a round on payment of a usually modest green fee.

Many New Zealanders who enjoy yachting embarked on the sport in their youth, in boats that are little more than dinghys with a mast. These boys (right) are launching their boat at Port Taranaki, dominated by one of the large offshore rigs which have been searching for gas and oil off the Taranaki coast.

For many years, the rest of New Zealand thought of Taranaki only as "cow cocky" (dairy farmer) land. The province remains one of New Zealand's premier dairying areas, but the discovery of oil and gas reserves, on shore and off, have given Taranaki new status as the country's "energy province". Watching over all the recent industrial activity, including the plant on the Kapuni gas field (opposite), is the almost perfect cone of the mountain which is sacred to the Maori as Taranaki but was renamed by Captain Cook Mount Egmont. Though lower, at 2518 metres, than Japan's Fujiyama Taranaki's sweep up from almost level farmland and the sea is quite as majestic.

N orth of Wellington, the coastal plain of the Manawatu and Horowhenua runs up against the steep hill country which guards the approaches to the country's capital, Wellington. The hills were formidable barriers to travellers, but today broad highways and railway tunnels make it feasible for commuters to live in Paekakariki (right), the first town on the coastal plain, or even further north, and travel in to Wellington to work.

Years ago, the Wanganui River (opposite top) was known as "The Rhine of Maoriland" and a journey down its gorged upper reaches by riverboat was on every tourist's itinerary. Today the river is regaining tourist popularity. Canoe or jetboat trips on its upper reaches, from Taumarunui down to Pipiriki or Jerusalem have again opened the river's grand beauty up for tourists. At the river's mouth, Wanganui is one of the oldest of the country's secondary centres (it was founded in 1840). In the city which flourishes today on each side of the river's last gentle loops towards the Tasman Sea are many interesting old buildings and a fine museum and art gallery.

The lower half of the North Island is dominated geographically by the high, rugged mountains of the Rimutuka, Tararua and Ruahine Ranges which separate the east coast from the west. The ranges themselves remain bushed and offer excellent walking and tramping. The hill country on each side of the ranges has mostly been cleared and is now farmed. Nosing up back roads, like this one in the Pohangina Valley (opposite below), which ramble across the broken country of attractive farmland is one of the pleasures of independent travel in New Zealand.

The architecture of Wellington's older houses has delighted generations of visitors to the city. The inner suburb of Thorndon (left) has been rescued in recent years from blight and decay and a vigorous local precinct society ensures that its historical character and charm are preserved, even though the vigorous rebuilding of downtown Wellington and the building of motorways have at times threatened the neighbourhood.

New Zealand has a thriving and creative craft pottery business. Hundreds of potters, all through the country, produce work which can be bought "at the gate" (the sign "Pottery" is commonplace on New Zealand highways) or in urban craft shops. Here potter Smicek (above) who works near Waikanae is loading his kiln for firing.

New Zealand cities are now well-endowed with world-class concert chambers. Christchurch has had its Town Hall since the 1970s and Auckland is completing its Aotea Centre. The auditorium of Wellington's Michael Fowler Centre (right), modelled on Christchurch's Town Hall, has drawn world-renowned performers to Wellington's Arts Festival. It also provides a venue for such local performing arts groups as the New Zealand Symphony Orchestra.

The waters of Wellington Harbour are often calm, but the city straddles south over hills to touch the shores of tempestuous Cook Strait. At Lyall Bay(opposite top), not far from Wellington's carrier-like airport, a boardrider exhilarates in the fine surf generated by powerful southerly swells.

New Zealanders are inveterate spectators of sports, and even the televising of matches has not emptied the stands at Wellington's Basin Reserve (opposite below) where cricket holds sway through the summer months. Despite its small population, New Zealand holds its own in many sports and in rugby regularly claims the world crown.

Wellington is built on often precipitous hills and its roads writhe up steep slopes to reach the higher suburbs. The suburb of Kelburn can be reached by road, but the more romantic way is on the Kelburn cable car (top), opened in 1902 but upgraded and provided with new cars in 1979. The short, inexpensive ride takes visitors to a fine viewpoint 122 metres above the city. This is now the sole surviving cable car in New Zealand. Dunedin's once more extensive system was scrapped not long after the Second World War.

New Zealand began building a grand new Parliament Buildings soon after the First World War, but the project was abandoned, half-finished, in the early 1920s. For years the government of New Zealand was housed in an inadequate, incomplete structure. When the need for new accommodation became urgent, the Government asked a noted British architect, Basil Spence, to suggest how the Parliament Buildings might be completed. The result was a new Executive Wing, completed in 1981, which was quickly nicknamed The Beehive (bottom). With the 19th century General Assembly Library, the half-finished Parliament House of the 1920s and the later Beehive, New Zealand's Parliament Buildings now form an interesting precinct of old and new buildings.

TOWNS AND WILDERNESS
Nelson, Marlborough and Westland

Looking north across Cook Strait, South Islanders often refer to themselves as "mainlanders". Once the South Island was New Zealand's "mainland" — when Otago's and Westland's gold and Canterbury's wool earned the country the best part of its wealth. But this was last century. Today political and economic power in New Zealand lie to the north of the narrow strait which separates the two islands.

But two facts give substance to a claim that the South is the more important island. In area the South Island is somewhat larger than the North. More significantly, the South Island boasts the country's most spectacular scenery. The Southern Alps, the Southern Lakes and Fiordland — everything is on a grander scale down south, except the cities and towns.

Human communities on the South Island are small and separated from each other by great distances of mountainous country or sparsely populated farm land. Dunedin and Christchurch, the South Island's main cities, are substantially smaller than Auckland or Wellington. There is more of a sense still on the South Island of humanity having a tenuous hold on the land. The typical views are of mountains, rising higher than the bushline, seen across empty plains or past isolated farmhouses.

North Islanders look more to the sea, South Islanders to the mountains, for their leisure pursuits and visitors to New Zealand can expect quite different experiences and activities once they have crossed Cook Strait.

In Nelson, Marlborough and Westland, the northern and western fringes of the South Island, the sense of small cities and towns sitting precariously on a still wild land is particularly pronounced. Nelson City is warm, sunny and settled, with pleasant beaches, but it is separated from the rest of the South Island by rugged mountains.

Nelson's neighbour to the east, Marlborough, is also separated from Canterbury by rugged ranges and is tied into the rest of the South Island by a sometimes fragile road and rail link down the wild east coast. But the top end of Marlborough frays into the complicated, often calm, waterways of the Marlborough Sounds, where the sea rules life and leisure as it does in Auckland.

Westland is even more a world unto itself than Nelson or Marlborough. Separated from Canterbury by the high main backbone of the Southern Alps and from Nelson by rough mountains and deep gorges, Westland has a sparse population. But the relatively few Coasters give their long, narrow province a stronger regional identity than almost any other part of New Zealand.

The rainfall is notorious, but when the sun is shining, Westland can be magical with icy peaks rising above forested ranges and wild rushing rivers. A fascinating past of gold mining, timber milling and coal mining has given Westland a legacy of historic buildings and relics which is, for visitors, the icing on the scenic cake.

A flight from Wellington to Christchurch takes little more than half an hour. By surface, the journey takes a full day, a journey which begins with a four-hour ferry ride, across Cook Strait and through the sheltered waterways of Tory Channel and Queen Charlotte Sound to the port of Picton. Here a ferry is on the last stretch of the journey into Picton near the head of Queen Charlotte Sound. Cook named the Sound after England's Queen and had a favourite anchorage in its outer reaches. The Maori before him had found the Sounds an appealing place to live and on the headland which the ferry is passing are the remains of an old pa or fortified village.

The rocky stretch of coast which separates Tasman and Golden Bays is protected as New Zealand's smallest national park. The park is named after the European discoverer of New Zealand, Abel Tasman, who anchored in Golden Bay in 1642. An unfortunate clash with local Maori resulted in Tasman's sailing away without landing, leaving four dead. The tall column on a hill above Tata Beach (above) is a monument to Tasman.

The Marlborough Sound's labyrinth of waterways — they are valleys drowned by the sea — are a holiday paradise to many people from Wellington, Nelson, Blenheim and Christchurch. Holiday cottages stand on the shores of many bays, like Ketu Bay (right). Some of these bays can be reached only by sea. Pleasure boats frequent the calm waters which holiday makers also use for both swimming and fishing.

The coastline of the Abel Tasman National Park (it was proclaimed in 1942, 300 years after Tasman's visit) is not dramatic, but has its own distinctive beauty. Sandy beaches alternate with rocky points and islets stud the coastal waters. It is a place to relax or walk without too much exertion, like this party in the hills behind Anchorage (above).

The golden yellow flowers of the kowhai (right) brighten many New Zealand landscapes in spring. In different habitats the kowhai grows as a prostrate shrub or tall tree. Its bright flowers have made it a favourite garden tree.

Nelson faces north, towards the sun, and its mild climate has attracted retired people to the city. It has also fostered a large fruit-growing industry. Apples predominate, but other crops, including cherries (opposite), are picked through the summer by a small army of seasonal workers. Nelson has an unhurried, almost "laid-back" atmosphere which has attracted many craftspeople and those seeking "alternative" life styles.

Even rain has not deterred these eager catchers of the delicacy whitebait at the mouth of a small river, the Kahutara (left), just south of Kaikoura. The South Island's east coast is often inhospitable and the rivers cut a swift passage through banked-up shingle into the South Pacific. But the river mouths are popular with people who like to fish, whether for tiny whitebait or large sea-run salmon.

Between Blenheim and Christchurch — a distance of 320 kilometres along the South Island's wild east coast — only Kaikoura is a settlement of any size. The town serves farmers of the district and fishermen who work out of the town's little port. The Kaikoura Ranges (above) press close to the coast, crowding road and rail to a narrow coastal strip. It is one of New Zealand's most scenic main routes.

The West Coast of the South Island, on the windward side of the Southern Alps, receives more than its fair share of rain. But though wet, the Coast's climate is relatively mild and nikau palms (above) give a subtropical look to the coastline between Westport and Greymouth, just north of Punakaiki's Pancake Rocks.

New Zealand's newest national park, the Paparoa National Park, protects both the high Paparoa Range itself and the unique lowland, but rugged, limestone terrain on the west coast. At Punakaiki (left), the limestone has been eroded by the sea into the Pancake Rocks, below which the sea surges in deep caverns and holes, a spectacular sight when a heavy swell is running.

The largest town on the West Coast, Greymouth (right), is situated (as its name makes obvious) at the mouth of the Grey River. Stone breakwaters were built to create a river port on a coast which lacks natural harbours, but crossing the bar is hazardous and most of the West Coast's timber and coal is sent east along the Midland Railway, through the eight-and-a-half kilometre long Otira Tunnel to Canterbury. Parts of downtown Greymouth stand on the site of the Mawhera Pa — the Maori before the European finding the river mouths the best places for their settlements.

W estland confronts the Tasman Sea with an inhospitable coastline whose wild shingle beaches are broken only by the mouths of the rivers and occasional rocky bluffs. The Arahura River (above) reaches the sea between Greymouth and Hokitika. It is a river with a special mana or standing, because from it was obtained most of the pounamu or greenstone which was the most prized of all stones for ornaments, weapons and implements by the pre-European Maori. In summer, parties would cross the Southern Alps to carry greenstone back to the east coast. The tough, hard stone occurs in the mountains from which the Arahura River flows.

Today, much of the greenstone recovered from the Arahura River is worked in Hokitika itself by tradesmen and craftsmen producing ornaments and jewellery for visitors (right). A traditional Maori influence is often evident, even in pieces of modern design and execution.

Like the Arahura River, the Taramakau River (opposite), reaches the sea between Greymouth and Hokitika. The upper reaches of the Taramakau provided a route into Westland for the gold diggers of the 1860s. Escaping from the mountains, the river crosses a narrow coastal plain, pauses in a lagoon, then escapes to the sea.

The townships at Fox Glacier and Franz Josef are only a few hundred metres above sea level, surrounded by bush-covered ranges. From them the visitor can be whisked by skiplane to the stark world of permanent snowfield and ice-bound rock where the glaciers have their birth. Here visitors are on the snowfields at the head of the Fox Glacier (above), close to the formidable west faces of Mount Tasman, New Zealand's second highest peak.

Even mountaineers now use skiplanes to avoid the back-breaking labour of carrying heavy packs up rock ridges to gain the high snowfields. But the planes can only land in certain places and there are heights that can only be reached by strenuous effort. These two climbers, roped together for safety in a world of deep, often hidden, crevasses, are toiling up a snowfield towards the summit of a peak above the Fox neve (left).

In South Westland, the Central Alps loom high above a narrow coastal strip and the transition from grassy flats to snowy summits is dramatically abrupt. The river flats of the coastal plain at places like Whataroa (top) are farmed, but the high rainfall makes it hard for farmers to keep their farm buildings from looking neglected. To many, this adds to the rustic charm of the West Coast.

$\mathbf{I}$n South Westland, vast snowfields beneath New Zealand's highest peaks feed the Franz Josef and Fox Glaciers, which force their way down below the bushline. Though the glaciers have retreated dramatically in recent decades, they remain impressive sights, whether seen from a distance out on the river flats (this view (top) is of the Fox Glacier from the Fox River flats) or close up. The energetic can walk to the ice of the lower glaciers. Helicopters lift the less active to fine vantage points above the contorted icefalls.

The West Coast's high rainfall encourages the growth of some of the densest forest in New Zealand (above). Much forest has been felled for timber, but much has survived and bush tracks provide enchanting walks through genuine rain forest. Coasters insist they see as much sunshine as the rest of the country, and the tracks can often be enjoyed in pleasant weather. But when it does rain on the West Coast, it really rains.

The view of the high alps from Lake Matheson (right), near Fox Glacier, is one of the most photographed views in New Zealand. But justly so, for the view is superb in its many moods and a refreshing sight when seen for the first or the fifty-first time.

MOUNTAIN AND PLAIN
Canterbury

Canterbury is the most populous of the South Island's six provinces. Christchurch, its capital city, is easily the South Island's largest concentration of people, not far in fact behind Wellington. Nevertheless, Canterbury is still a province of great open spaces. In much of the province, the only signs of human occupation are lonely farm houses on broad plains and even lonelier homesteads in the dramatic high country. The contrast between the settled, civilised air of Christchurch and the empty, austere ranges of the interior is marked indeed.

The geographical and scenic contrasts which are typical of New Zealand as a whole are more marked in Canterbury than anywhere else in the country. The Canterbury Plains — more than 150 kilometres from north to south and up to 40 kilometres broad at their widest point — are New Zealand's largest area of flat lowland. But the province also boasts New Zealand's highest mountain, Cook or Aoraki, not to mention its largest glacier, the Tasman.

It is to the mountains, the drier front ranges and the snowy main chain of the Southern Alps, that people in Canterbury tend to look for their leisure and recreation. One reason for this is that much of the Canterbury coast is open and sometimes inhospitable beach, unsafe for swimming and uninviting for boating. Only in North Canterbury and, above all, in the sheltered harbours and inlets of Banks Peninsula are there stretches of coast which offer the opportunities for coastal and maritime pursuits which figure so prominently in North Island life.

The Canterbury high country, a broad belt of dry mountains and large intermontane basins, covered mostly with golden-fawn tussock grass and drained by great rivers with broad, braided beds of grey shingle, has a special place in New Zealand mythologies. The huge sheep runs and the lonely, adventuresome lives of musterers and drovers and of runowners' families have a special quality which fascinates "lowland" New Zealanders. It is an area of scenic splendour with its snow and rock peaks rising high above the grey, gravelly river beds and golden tussock hills.

Travellers reaching Canterbury from the North Island will find here, as elsewhere in the South, a more unhurried pace of life. The cities, even Christchurch, still have more of a small-town atmosphere, and even appearance, than the larger cities and towns of the North. They are qualities of life which persuade many South Islanders not to join the drift to the north which has been occurring for most of this century. Added to the South Island's undoubtedly more magnificent scenery, they are reasons for travellers to explore the different, but still very varied, experiences of Canterbury's wide open spaces.

When the first European settlers reached the site of Christchurch more than 130 years ago, the Avon River flowed sluggishly between banks thick with raupo, flax and niggerheads. Today woodland and garden in riverbank parks like the Millbrook Reserve (left) contribute to Christchurch's established, perhaps English, air. Relaxing on lawns which slope down to a rippling stream is a distinctively Christchurch pleasure.

Christchurch (above), founded at the end of 1850, has an old established air which has prompted many visitors to compare it with English towns. Despite the recent building boom which has transformed the skyline of downtown Christchurch, a remarkable legacy of older Gothic, grey-stone buildings still sets the city's architectural character. An important cluster of these buildings, five minutes walk from the Square at the city's centre, includes the Arts Centre, in the foreground. The Arts Centre came into existence in the 1970s after the University of Canterbury had abandoned its central city site for a new suburban campus. Shops, galleries, craft workshops and theatres now occupy the university's fine old buildings. A thriving weekend market has become a major Christchurch attraction. Beyond the venerable old buildings and fine trees of Christchurch is the distant line of the snowclad "foothills" of the Southern Alps, though in most other countries they would rate as mountains not hills. The intriguing juxtaposition of civilisation and wild nature is more marked in Canterbury than in other parts of New Zealand.

New Zealand life is not all a matter of vigorous, outdoor pursuits. More leisurely, artistic, usually indoor pursuits play as important a part in the lives of many New Zealanders as sport. Several of New Zealand's leading craft weavers are based in Canterbury (far left), appropriately for a province which has counted fine wool among its major products since the 1850s. The products of craft looms are sought eagerly by businesses and individuals.

A recent touch which has enhanced Christchurch's reputation as an "English" city has been the introduction of punts onto the Avon River (left). The punts can be hired for leisurely journeys between city hotels, restaurants and other attractions, including the Town Hall, built in the 1970s on a prime riverfront site.

When provincial and international teams clash on Christchurch's Lancaster Park (above), crowds of tens of thousands flock to watch the games. New Zealanders now play a great variety of individual and team sports, but cricket and rugby, traditionally the main two male games, continue to enjoy large followings. Lancaster Park is typical of many in the country on which both sports are played, depending on the season.

Like most Canterbury beaches, Waimairi (opposite top) faces the open sea. Some Canterbury beaches are shingle and shelve steeply, but the beaches north of Banks Peninsula are sandy and shelve more gently, providing summer swimming. But swimming from the open beaches is not always safe and surf lifesaving clubs provide an extra margin of safety. Surf carnivals are important events for those who, many of them volunteers, make sure their fellow citizens can swim in safety. But North Island participants in carnivals like this sometimes complain that the South Island's water is unacceptably cold.

Joggers, running solitary or in pairs or packs, are a familiar sight in most New Zealand cities. In Christchurch a lunchtime circuit of Hagley Park is a favourite pursuit of active city workers. Once a year (opposite right) the city's runners mass in Cathedral Square for a run of several kilometres (it degenerates into a leisurely walk for some) out to New Brighton, one of Christchurch's seaside suburbs.

Among the more unusual sports played in New Zealand, reflecting the country's predominantly British heritage, is polo. This game sees the North Island pitted against the South during Christchurch's Show Weekend (right), when the annual agricultural and pastoral show and a public holiday give the city a relaxed, almost carnival atmosphere.

The river flats and hillsides of the Canterbury high country have been grazed since the European occupation of the South Island. Sheep have predominated, particularly the hardy merino, but cattle also graze high country pastures, like this herd of Hereford beef cattle being forced across the Clarence River (top).

In spring and early summer, Canterbury's flocks are mustered down to woolsheds for an annual shearing (above). Here shearers and shedhands are hard at work on the Northbank Station, near Rakaia. Canterbury's woolsheds (most built of timber and corrugated iron) range from tiny two or three stand sheds to large buildings which survive from the days of the great runs in which twenty or thirty sheep can be shorn at one time. Canterbury offers opportunities to stay on or visit working farms.

Christchurch is an important manufacturing centre, but along with Canterbury's other larger towns — Ashburton and Timaru to the south and Kaiapoi and Rangiora to the north — it seems more dependent still on its rural hinterland than most North Island cities. The plains and downlands of Canterbury (right) afford attractive rural landscapes. Cropping and horticulture are important in Canterbury, but meat and wool from lambs and sheep are still pre-eminent in a province which gave its name to "Canterbury lamb" last century.

The jetboat is a New Zealand invention. A high country run-holder, pondering how to run a boat on the shallow, shingle-bedded rivers of the eastern South Island like the Godley (opposite), hit on the simple expedient of drawing water in beneath the boat and expelling it at the rear. The jetboat can skim through shallow water and ride easily up swift rapids.

Salmon were introduced into New Zealand last century and runs up the rivers of the South Island's east coast draw anglers in large numbers. Here at the mouth of Canterbury's largest river, the Rakaia (above), fishermen have taken up their positions in a continuous fence on the river's shingle banks. Salmon are now farmed in many places in New Zealand. This has put salmon onto New Zealand menus, but robbed the fish of some of the glamour it had when the only salmon served were fish plucked from cold rushing waters by individual anglers.

Cold blue lakes are an attractive feature of many Canterbury high country landscapes. A stiff nor'-west wind blowing down from the Southern Alps sends this wind surfer scudding across the choppy surface of Lake Clearwater (right).

(Over page, left) Canterbury's high country is renowned for the clarity and brilliance of its light, shining here across a crop being grown on irrigated land, with tussock covered hills and the dark line of a windbreak beyond. In the high country occur greater extremes of climate than are common in New Zealand. Heavy snow (over page, right top) can lie on the ground for weeks and savage frosts freeze and turn white landscapes which in high summer were golden under a scorching sun. In the Cass Valley (over page, right middle) autumn brings a flare of bright yellow as a birch tree turns with the season. The small hut is typical of those built primarily for the men who muster the high country pastures. Through summer, exotic lupins on the shores of Lake Tekapo (over page, right bottom) introduce a touch of bright colour into a landscape which is otherwise austere, characterised by greys, fawns and browns.

Skiing is to the South Island what sailing is to the North. Most of the country's skifields, and certainly its finest, are on the South Island. The fields range from small club fields to large commercial fields which offer full facilities, including chairlifts and restaurants. The commercial fields offer exhilarating skiing (right) on slopes of packed snow. But one of the country's most exciting skiing experiences is to be lifted by skiplane onto the vast snowfields at the head of the Tasman Glacier (above) to ski down virgin snow over broad slopes or through icefalls and seracs. The introduction of heliskiing has opened even more remote virgin snowfields to adventuresome skiers.

The largest of the Mackenzie Country lakes is Pukaki and the view across this lake to the "roof of New Zealand" (opposite) includes New Zealand's two highest peaks, Cook and Tasman. The lake's steep shingle banks are evidence of its use to store water to generate electricity. The Mackenzie Country is the largest of Canterbury's intermontane basins and its scenery is on a magnificent scale.

84

SOUTHERN GRANDEUR
Otago and Southland

wo provinces lie south of the Waitaki River. Southlanders may dislike being 'lumped in' with Otago, but in the days of provincial government last century, Southland enjoyed only brief independence from Otago. Today the eastern coastal regions of the South Island from Oamaru to Invercargill form one broadly similar region. The towns and cities are comfortable and established but have not enjoyed much growth in recent years. The hill country and plains are neatly farmed, though here and there patches of wilder country remain for contrast, for example in the Catlins. The people share the strong Scottish traditions of southern New Zealand, tending to be slower of speech and perhaps more reserved than people from further north.

Coastal Otago and Southland may share many similarities, but the two provinces have very different interiors — Central Otago and Fiordland. An exciting past as one of New Zealand's major 19th century goldfields gives historic interest to the massive ranges and broad valleys of Central Otago. Its landscapes are dramatic. Great rivers swirl between dry hills and through rock-bound gorges. The blocky schist mountains cradle some of New Zealand's finest lakes. Fantastic tors of wind-weathered schist stud high, lonely moors. Central Otago's winters can be as cold as its summers are hot and heavy winter snow on the mountains provides some of the best skiing in the country.

The lakes and rivers of Central Otago not only enhance the region's scenery; they also provide opportunities for exciting forms of boating. Queenstown, on Lake Wakatipu, is one of the country's major tourist centres. The region is farmed, but there is little cultivation. Herds of sheep and cattle range the dry hills or are concentrated on more productive pastures where irrigation water flows. In the river valleys are grown some of New Zealand's finest stone fruits.

Fiordland, a national park of more than one million hectares, occupies all of western Southland. It is close to Central Otago, but vastly different from it. The hard rock mountains are almost unbelievably steep and a heavy rainfall sustains a luxuriant forest cover. Within living memory the word "unexplored" was written across great tracts of Fiordland. In 1948 a bird thought extinct for decades, the takahe, was rediscovered in a high, remote valley.

Today, Fiordland is better known and more accessible. A good road leads from Te Anau through the Homer Tunnel and down to Milford Sound, the most impressive of the fiords that have given the region its name, and the Manapouri power scheme has opened Doubtful Sound to visitors.

Two lakes — Te Anau, the South Island's largest, and Manapouri, thought by many to be New Zealand's most beautiful — lie on the eastern edges of Fiordland. West of the lakes are the rugged mountains, steep-walled valleys and dramatic waterways of the fiords themselves whose scenic grandeur has helped earn world heritage status for the South Island's south-western regions.

Central Otago's lakes come in all sizes, shapes and colours. Not far from long, narrow and large Lake Wakatipu is small, almost round Lake Hayes (left), which shares with its neighbour the setting of scenic grandeur that made "The Southern Lakes" famous as long ago as last century.

Beautifully situated on a bay on the north shore of sinuous Lake Wakatipu, Queenstown is the hub of Central Otago's thriving tourist industry. As an international centre, Queenstown boasts an impressive array of shops and restaurants, the envy of many other New Zealand centres, even larger ones. A profusion of dried flowers, grasses and fruits in the Flower Barn (opposite) make a colourful display.

Evidence of Central Otago's romantic goldmining past is found throughout the region, but nowhere is that past recalled more pleasantly or completely than at Arrowtown (top), a small town on the banks of the swift Arrow River from which fabulous amounts of gold were taken last century. Arrowtown has preserved many of its attractive old buildings from goldmining days and is making valiant efforts to ensure that development does not harm the town's special character. A row of old cottages beneath now tall exotic trees may be New Zealand's most photographed buildings.

Four steamers once plied the waters of Lake Wakatipu. Now only the "Earnslaw" (bottom) remains, known affectionately as The Lady of the Lake. The 51-metre long twin screw steamer was prefabricated in Dunedin and assembled at Kingston in 1912. Her main work now is carrying summer visitors to Queenstown for a trip on the lake, but she continues also to provide a regular service for lakeside runholders whose properties cannot be reached by road.

Queenstown (above) has grown fast in recent years as people have flocked to the town as a centre for skiing in winter on nearby fields, for a host of water sports and activities in summer and for enjoyment of superb scenery all the year round. Queenstown glows at dusk like a large, sophisticated resort, but it has grown without losing entirely its charming, small town atmosphere.

The impressive mountain country around Queenstown was once alive with intrepid miners seeking gold. Today it is scenery, not gold, which brings people into these same, now lonely, mountains, like these horse trekkers (right) near Moonlight.

90

As a mountainous land of plentiful rainfall, New Zealand has many tempestuous rivers which fall steeply, brawling over boulders or crashing fiercely between rocks. The jetboat was first developed to cope with the shallow, braided shingle rivers of Canterbury, but proved to have mastery also over the deeper, swift and treacherous rivers of Central Otago. A ride by jetboat on the Shotover River (left) is a highlight of many visits to Queenstown. The rafters (above) are being thrilled by their fast, bumpy descent of a Central Otago river. Commercial operators on both islands run trips which allow the inexperienced to enjoy in safety the thrills of white water.

New Zealand has more than a dozen vintage working railways. The most famous of all the steam trains still running is the Kingston Flyer (left), named after a crack express which once ran from Gore to Kingston but is now confined to a short stretch of track.

The real wealth of Central Otago today does not come from gold — almost all the gold there was to win has already been recovered — and not even from the thousands of visitors who flock to Queenstown, Wanaka and other tourist centres. It comes rather from the flocks and herds which graze the region's rough hill country and its improved pastures. Sheep (right) are the longest established in the area, then came cattle, followed recently by deer (above). The variety of stock adds to the region's interest for visitors.

Queenstown's restaurants, boutiques and nightspots give it some of its appeal to visitors. But it is above all the natural grandeur of the long lake on which it stands that makes Queenstown a special place. Across the lake from Queenstown are two venerable sheep stations — Mount Nicholas (left) and Walter Peak — to which visitors can escape from Queenstown's urban delights to a world of rural pursuits and scenic magnificence.

The eastern shore of Lake Te Anau (below) is relatively smooth and near the town of Te Anau almost treeless. But to the west and north, the lake probes long fiords deep into lofty ranges whose flanks are heavily forested. The lake offers days of exploration of its wooded islands, myriad bays and forested coves to those lucky enough to own boats, like these moored on the town's waterfront. Public launch trips ensure that visitors without their own boats can enjoy New Zealand's second largest lake in the same way.

Guarding the head of the Hollyford Valley and blocking the way through to Milford Sound is the solid rock of Mount Talbot (right), pocket glaciers perched on its steep flanks. The Homer Tunnel was pierced through this formidable rock wall to give access to Milford Sound, previously accessible only by foot (along the Milford Track) or sea. Work began on the tunnel in 1935 but the one-way tunnel was not completed until 1952.

In Fiordland are two of the most popular alpine walking tracks in New Zealand — the Milford and Routeburn Tracks. Other tracks or routes in the Fiordland National Park are more difficult. Only the more adventuresome, and the better equipped and more highly skilled, attempt such crossings as Gertrude Saddle (left), where this party has pitched its idyllic camp.

The kea (top) is a world oddity — the only parrot at home in truly alpine environments. An inquisitive, mischievous bird, it has been accused, wrongly many think, of killing sheep. Arthur's Pass and the Homer Tunnel portal are two places where visitors can see kea. The flash of red underwing as it flies overhead and its raucous call are loved by all who frequent the Southern Alps.

The tough, hard rock of the Fiordland mountains delights climbers who have coped with the shattered, unreliable greywackes of ranges further north. The Darran Mountains (above), north of Milford Sound, are a particular mecca for New Zealand's athletic rockclimbers and for the increasing numbers of climbers from overseas who come to test their skills on the varied terrain and differing conditions of the Southern Alps.

Hundreds of New Zealand families own their own small jetboats and in summer tow them behind the family car to rivers and lakes throughout the country. Campers on the shore of Fiordland's Mavora Lakes (right) have brought their boats with them to make the most of their lakeside holiday.

Near vertical walls of rock, towering from water that plunges nearly three hundreds metre deep, to a summit, Mitre Peak, more than 1200 metres high — the drama of Milford Sound (below) has impressed visitors since last century. On a pocket handkerchief of flat land at the head of the Sound is a hotel and other facilities for visitors, the terminus of the road from Te Anau. The energetic reach Milford Sound by walking the Milford Track, "the finest walk in the world".

One of the popular walking tracks in the south-west of the South Island is the Routeburn, from the head of Lake Wakatipu to the Milford Road. For part of its length, the Routeburn Track sidles high on a mountainside above the bushline, with spectacular views of the Darran Mountains across the depths of the Hollyford Valley (opposite).

The country's longest no-exit road runs from the town of Te Anau to Milford Sound. The dramatic sound is the spectacular culmination of a journey rated one of the finest alpine drives in the world. Mountains tower above stately valleys and untouched forest, and lofty waterfalls tumble into attractive lakes. At The Divide (between the Eglinton and Hollyford Valleys) a short walk takes the energetic visitor to bush-fringed Lake McKellar (above).

At Balclutha, south of Dunedin, the main railway line and road down the east coast of the South Island turns inland to Gore before turning south again towards Invercargill. Another road to Invercargill twists round the indented coastline where the block of hill country occupying the south-east corner of the Island runs down to the sea. This is the Catlins, an area little known even to many New Zealanders although it is an area of considerable if not dramatic scenic beauty. These falls at Purakanui (right) are one of the area's attractions.

104

Tuatapere, west of Invercargill on the banks of the Waiau River, with a population of fewer than one thousand, serves farms of the Waiau Valley but it is also a timber town. It stands on the edge of untamed Fiordland and still has the air of a frontier town. At a carnival in the town on New Years Day, the masculine ethos of pioneering New Zealand still finds expression in such competitions as wood chopping and a tug-of-war (left and opposite).

A rough road along the shores of Lake Wakatipu leads to the town of Glenorchy (above) at the Lake's head, where two rivers flow down magnificent valleys into the lake. A small town, which for most of its life was accessible only by lake steamer, Glenorchy, the starting off point for the popular Routeburn Track, is the site of the headquarters of the Mount Aspiring National Park. The township is famous for its summer race meeting, a far cry from the huge crowds in grandstands at major urban courses, but perhaps more enjoyable for jockeys and spectators alike.

South of the hills which surround Dunedin is one of Otago's few extensive areas of flat land, the Taieri Plain. The lowest parts of the plain are occupied by placid Lake Waihola, (above) where a young fisherman bends his rod in the pure evening light that is one of the glories of the South Island and which gives its fine landscapes an often magical luminosity.

Otago Harbour (right) reaches into the heart of the Otago Peninsula. The harbour attracted Scottish settlers who founded the city of Dunedin, their 'Edinburgh of the South', at its head in 1848. Closer to the harbour's entrance, nearer deep water, Port Chalmers provides container berths that carry Otago's produce to distant ports. Like Oamaru to its north, Dunedin has grown only imperceptibly in recent years, slowly indeed since the years of giddy growth after the Otago goldrushes which made it briefly New Zealand's most important city. The setting of sea and hill and the legacy of old buildings resulting from past prosperity and later stagnation make Dunedin one of New Zealand's most appealing cities for visitors with an interest in history and architecture.

The Maori explained the presence of curious spherical boulders on the beach at Moeraki (opposite), just south of Oamaru by telling of the wreck of the ancestral canoe Araiteuru on nearby Shag Point and of the drifting ashore of circular foodbaskets. The story is more romantic than the geological truth that they are concretions formed on the seafloor millions of years ago. But the Maori legend has appealed to generations of young New Zealanders who have been intrigued by the perfect roundness of the boulders.

Bluff (top) takes its name from the knobbly hill which protrudes from the southern coast of the South Island into the often rough waters of Foveaux Strait. It is a port town, Southland's only outlet for the products of its rich pastures. Across the harbour, on Tiwai Point, an aluminium smelter consumes electricity generated at Lake Manapouri. Bluff is a windswept town, fascinating for the feeling it gives of being an outpost. And indeed south of Bluff are only Stewart Island, a scattering of subantarctic islands and then the icy seas of Antarctica.

Oamaru (middle), just across the provincial 'frontier' of the Waitaki River, is the guardian of Otago's northern approaches. It has given its name to a building stone, a white, easily carved limestone, which was used extensively throughout New Zealand. Stone from Oamaru's quarries was used for many of the town's own buildings and as 'Whitestone City' it is being increasingly recognised for the quality of its late 19th and early 20th century architecture. The town's slow growth in recent years — the port is no longer open — has helped many of these buildings to survive.

New Zealand's many rivers were formidable barriers to communications when the first settlers arrived. River ferries are now mostly a thing of the past in New Zealand, but in the days before many bridges had been built, punts and other ferries provided vital links between communities. At Tuapeka Mouth on the Clutha River a punt (bottom) moved across the river by the force of the current is a reminder of those earlier times.

111

Only the adventure-some reach New Zealand's last tiny outpost of civilisation, the small settlement of Oban on Stewart Island's Half-moon Bay. The Island is reached by a ferry that is little more than a large fishing boat and can roll alarmingly in the sometimes heavy seas of Foveaux Strait or by a small plane that touches down on a primitive (though sealed) ridge top air strip. Fewer than four hundred people live on Stewart Island, confined to a tiny stretch of the Island's 1600 kilometres of coastline. There are only a little more than twenty kilometres of formed road. Most of the Island's landscapes are wild and unmodified, but there are beautiful beaches and walking tracks through fine bush full of native birds. Easy tracks abound near the settlement, but much of the Island, like Port Pegasus in the far south (above), can be reached only by days of often arduous walking or by fishing boat.